THE RUB

THE RUB

ARIANA-SOPHIA KARTSONIS

ELIXIR PRESS / DENVER

PUBLISHED BY ELIXIR PRESS

P.O. Box 27029
Denver, Colorado 80227
www.elixirpress.com

Library of Congress Cataloging-in-Publication Data

Kartsonis, Ariana-Sophia M., 1966-
[Poems. Selections]
The rub / Ariana-Sophia Kartsonis.
p. cm
ISBN 1-932418-53-9 (acid-free paper)
I. Title.

PS3611.A7848A6 2014
811'.6—dc23
2014020045

Cover image, "Cricket, Princely Cricket," by Jean Cody
Cover design by Gilbert Mitchell Lear
Interior design by Alban Fischer
Author photo by Angela Fortin/afsphotos.com

10 9 8 7 6 5 4 3 2 1
FIRST EDITION

For my husband, Mitch:
>In thanks for our Goode life,
>our Hubcap Heaven, our funny little family
>and the so-worth-itness of that long wait.
>Glockenspiel Baby, *I'm satisfied and tickled too,*
>*just to be with you.*

CONTENTS

I

Pinocchio's Elegy for the Unreal 13

Where Secret Animals Graze 15

Jerusalem Rose Cafe 18

Soufflé 19

Manifesto of the Oven Mitt 20

Caribou 21

Elegy in the Form of Love Letter for the Missing Green Mountain Bike (Now) Known as the (Lost) Esmerelda Who Spins & Leaps Curbs & Creeks Somewhere in the Backroads of my Memory (& with Apologies to Glen Campbell) 23

Blown Glass 25

Heart Pine 27

Thirst 28

~Ode to Tilde 29

One Dummy Responds to the Once-Marionette 30

Last Leg 31

II

Caravan Cinderblock Fairytale 35

About the Other Animals 37

Sleeping Beauty Wakes to an Empty Bedroom 39

Enter Ophelia 40

Bodies That Hold Us 41

Reincarnated, Lot's Wife Carries Snapshots of Changed Skyline 43

Jivin' Ophelia Through the Afterlife of Broken Love 45

I'm the Mimi 46

Boycotting the Planetarium 48

I Love the Real World Because It Is an Achievement to Get There 49

Sidereal Time 50

Wishing Bone Spell to End Emptiness at Twilight or the Bed's Expanse or Rage at a Cloud
    Shaped Like the Trunk of a Muscular Man 51

Every Other Day Aubade 53

Piñata Grove 57

Charm for the Drowned Boy 59

The Rub 60

Last Wish for the Dollmaker's Ghost 63

Tearing Away 65

Notes for How to Carry the Memory of the Body 68

RSVP for the Princess Regarding Her Marriage to the Pea 70

Fable Down to One Jar Full of Feathers, a Murder, Some Murmuring of What Shouldn't Have
    to Die to Expect to Resurrect 72

Dearest Mistake 74

Octobering 75

Winter Interstice 76

Arachne Looks to the Scythe-Moon for a Light 77

Body Glitter 79

Ariadne 80

Gretel After Dark 82

For All My Bad Choices 84

III

Etiolation 89

Carillon 92

Riverside Driving Rain 93

Poem for My Tax-Man 95

One More for the Ghost of the Dollmaker's Ghost 96

Rohs Street 97

Phantom Ventriloquist Haiku 98

Furioso 99

Taking the Subway with Nadezdha Mandelstam 101

Charm for Inducing Razbliuto 104

Promenade 105

For Six Seconds 107

The Cricket is Her utmost
Of Elegy, to Me

EMILY DICKINSON

I

Here's the rub: you're on your own.
What breaks isn't replaceable anymore.

Gepetto's hand on your unhinged knee
won't set it right again. A torn

finger can't be carved anew.
You prayed for this: Real Boy,

then, at last, a skin of your own
to hide within. Real boy arms

are limp arms against a sea
of troubles. Now the stuff

you're carved from rots,
touches all it can then forgets

the touch. Not to mention pain,
broken skin and bones, the heavy

human heart and the way you get the part
where Hamlet says: *and by a sleep we end*

the heart-ache and the thousand natural
shocks that flesh is heir to.

This is for you Gepetto,
deep in the sleep of death.

Listen up Old Man (who once pulled my strings
knit the motion to my dance, tied to me

somewhere inside even now,
only I can't see the cables, can only feel their tug

like loss's magnetic field between memory and gut)
I miss the certainty of my ligneous hands.

Everything's either too far away or not enough.
I can still hear the toys talk, still hear the whispers

of the inanimate world, the soul of objects.
I wish you'd told me about the way it feels

to be watching life from a dying body.
Your workshop's veiled with cobwebs

every old tool dreams of your hands
your smoothing grip. In the corner

a spider unlaces a luna moth. A dinner
too huge too gossamer to be real.

WHERE SECRET ANIMALS GRAZE

Beside an open window, a bed.
A woman rises, stretches against
a pale sky. Her bent legs arch
to form a bridge over
the city. The outline of her
body becomes the skyline.

Beside the bed, her
shadow lies strewn
casually across the floor
where the forest of secret
animals collect in the rectangular
windowlight's Sanskrit of branch.
In the marrow of a tree's bare,
dry bones, secret birds sing strange
secret songs. The woman's hand pushes

her hair from her forehead.
In that motion, flocks scatter
from her shadow: secret
bats and nightowls and doves.
The spiders wait for her spread fingers
to leave a pattern on the floor then spin
a starry web, connecting points at each fingertip,
thread weaving across the palm.

The most secretive sleep under awning
of lampshade and curtain, tempted
to stir only when she performs shadowplays

on the wall: dinosaur or
antlered buck, a barking dog.

Meanwhile, mosaic giraffes wait
with the secret zebras and the wild,
secret stallions for a sign.
Behind the bureau, whole lakes
of secret fish swim in place,
while dark quiet mares sip the surface.

At night our hands: small, secret animals
search for secret shade, a place to nest:
whole jungles away from the woman in the city
and the brickwork buildings and the lives
within lives on the floors and ceilings
and walls of each room
with creatures at every turn.

Feeling behind the stars for signs of life
how would we know
that whole secret packs and tribes
gaze back from the outline cast
on the rug by a neck, a wrist, a reedy thigh?

Gloaming, overlooking the city, we believe,
see the moon rise and fall, rise again:
a second Venus, a drunken sun.

Like us, the woman in the room
sees something exquisite
to the growth of a forest.
The shaky stars. The tree's
covetous grasp for kite
or balloon. All the secret animals
she houses unawares. Bevy

and drove. Murder to murmuration,
gaggle to cry.

We believe in the hidden life
but we love our Cartesian charts,
our certain numbers, so we never see
the secret insects, never hear the silent mating
call of the secret wolves.

Even our flesh betrays, each line a map
in the world of organisms and parasites
we bed down with each night
in mattress fibers and eyelids.

On the fringe of a galaxy, one
of so many no less,
on the third floor, in a building across
town, a woman wakes.
A small universe sends
planets to the light source,
the secret larks begin.

JERUSALEM ROSE CAFE

I was forever dropping a flower in
the mail slot by the front door.
There, the Arab woman,
stooped a little,
makes my favorite dish:
chick peas and spinach and I love her.
A Jerusalem is the sweetest
artichoke of them all.
Now a sign on the front door
says *Closed for Medical Emergency
the week of November 10* and it's mid February
and I hear now that a Vietnamese joint
will open in the summer.
     Sometimes, too alone, I walk what sad
I can off to the grocery store
     and back by the barbershop.
Some candy hearts scattered at the bus stop
try to speak to me—something about
love and moving until you get to the next stop
but the only thing I can translate is HEY DOLL
or BABY ME. Every night I blow five kisses
westward from my balcony.
It's late afternoon before I turn down
the next block where the light is unfolding
in a million leaves of green. I am a spiral
of petals, a round loaf of bread dropped
into the sea, spinning and spinning
     with the hunger of a hundred sardines.

SOUFFLÉ

Five days into February, they're snowed-in
together for the first time. They are early
at this thing they've yet to name and she is thinking
about soufflés, how she knows nothing of how they're made
just how readily they fall. He recalls the bread factory
near his first apartment and the smell of what had to be
a promise in the air. She watches the snowflakes fall in braids:
ropes of double-helixed descent, and considers the patterns
things draw as they drop. For years he's thought nothing
about snowcreme: fresh snow, vanilla, sugar, and milk
in the dairy glass bottles, but today she remembers
the sweetness, the recipe for the way to take a weather in.

1. We intend to be there when there exists the demand for something better than your grandmother's quilt-square, threadbare potholder.

2. The essential elements of our design will be loyalty, sacrifice and humility.

3. We declare our allegiance to the stove, the occasional resentful foray to the backyard grill, where really a dishrag or hot pad would do. No long-suffering upside-down cake of a sun or sum of our days. Though we be mere mitts, we be mitts of a new kitchen.

4. There is no beauty in the doily. There is no excuse for the doily.

5. We include the aforementioned potholders and doilies with throw pillows and throw rugs. We adhere to the verb implicit in those modifiers. We sing loudly the praises of that s/he on the fifth floor terrace flinging furnishings to the winking street below.

6. We declare that if light and motion declare the solidity of objects then there can be no greater symbol of loyalty than the lowly oven mitt. Lament its forced hold of the human hand, the pot that holds the glorious soup that nourishes its oppressor. Let intimacy stand for that hand held to oven mitt, that scorch of pan to mitt holding heat meant for the sorry palms of their kind. Let all this be the concatenation of what we hold, holding us—taking the heat for what is meant to feed the hand that burns us in its stead.

CARIBOU

Passion Sunday and the wrong
season to be this doe dreaming you.
You, north American reindeer, you
light-tripping through some field or other.
I want to wear you, be worn by you;
nuzzle into that place between skin
and bone, nest there on holiday.
I even bought an Easter dress:
airy fabric, the color of hot chocolate,
of your hide, a velvet sash at the waist.
My hand dreams your velvet muzzle.
My fingers trail down your face
and I want to feed you passion
fruit, papaya, persimmon, pulpy mangos, sugar
plums, wild strawberries—*fraise sauvage*,
something fleshy-rich, un-needed.
When I can't sleep it's you
I'll count leaping your tinseled arch
over my bed and back again.

I would open you up, crawl in the husk
of you, live in the grey-brown skin of you
until it dissolved, would stay longer,
until your bones bleached white, until we
evaporated, dust-fine, mingled and scattered.
(I mean I'd hide in your hide if I could.)

Let me crawl in your pocket, wander the heart
of the deepest woods, sip from the same

stream, soar a December
night, rooftop landings, bells ringing, I want
the whole garland-draped lie.
I mean: let me stay.

Sunday morning and I'm on a plane bound
for nowhere-fast or anywhere-but-here.
Like you, Christmas beast, my timing's sadly-off.
You're a far cry from home
and I'm a long way off. I left you
a note that reads *they don't call you
Dasher for nothing*. But I'm not laughing.
By now you'd think we'd learn. Still, we wander
where we don't belong, find ourselves flying
fast on the wrong day in the wrong country
headlong into the wrong dream.
As if we care.

ELEGY IN THE FORM OF LOVE LETTER FOR THE MISSING GREEN MOUNTAIN
BIKE (NOW) KNOWN AS THE (LOST) ESMERELDA WHO SPINS & LEAPS CURBS
& CREEKS SOMEWHERE IN THE BACKROADS OF MY MEMORY
(& WITH APOLOGIES TO GLEN CAMPBELL)

When I say missing, I mean *stolen*.
When I say lost, I mean
me: the narrator, unmountained now,
wheel-less as any glacier.

O emeraldine skeleton
your spokes spin faster now,
I know it. When I see your twin, years
down the line, parked against
a bike rack three buildings away,
I see a rugged girl. If it is you there,
you are muddied for the first time, dinged some,
you have leapt things—water and stone.
Scarred a bit, and earning

your wildwest claim from the journey
from Utah to Alabama. You've surely kissed
the soil of both states now, the downtown
Salt Lake City darkgarden earth that makes

roses grow big as a truckdriver's head,
and that red Dixie clay ablush
with all its weird history. How does that dirt
taste to your tires? Me,

now, I haven't the heart even to drive
in my car to the bike shop where the big paper sign
in the window claims SALE.
I claimed you, o bike worthy of a name cribbed off

a gypsy woman from a novel (the same one
to give another Alabama girl-lost her name).
A summer day. My birthday present
to me. I bought you with cash

earned at a second job renting cabins
to skiers. I picked you up one afternoon,
and we coasted down a gold-plated hill.
We went to midnight movies in hottest July

and when I rode you home at two a.m.
to my air-conditionless apartment you threw
a dash of cool into that breeze
you tossed back to me. This poem

is a farewell kiss. A wave down the highway.
Without me now you can fly.

BLOWN GLASS

What was it? What is it? What will it be? We filled the world with our cry and calling.
—Czeslaw Milosz

Glass, glass, glass. Twin glass echoes in a glacier. Rain fell in sheets through a sleeveless
February, a bare-armed winter. We were there. Everything counted.

There's a wasp trapped in the window. In the light the wings are x-rays of wings. The honey-
paper body whispers between two panes of glass. I can't bring myself to rescue or destroy it.

Glassy shrieks pierced the glass globe made of a cat's-eye marble, three prayers and a late,
feverish winter. We were seven. Your hand went through the church window. Mama drove fast.
I held two petals of your skin together with both hands. Blood, purple-throated, operatic sang
through my fingers.

Seventy-three stitches. You bragged about it at recess. Years later slivers of
colored glass worked to the surface of your wrist. Blue, green, red. Sharp confetti.

That was the first night I dreamed glassmakers. Their grasp on the orange-lit metal rod, the
open-yawn of the fiery furnace, the shirtless men. Gasping heat. Gallons of melted glass.

You had a scar. From your wrist nearly to your elbow, snaking around in silkiest pink. A warped
corkscrew. You had a scar. I didn't. I cried, *We're supposed to be twins.*

I wish I'd never seen the molten glass pouring from the faucet, the cupped, thirsty hands.

Winter again. Music from somewhere. Blues. A cracked voice. *I'm so broke I can't even spend
the night.*

Flashback. You're running, laughing toward the house. We're all waiting in the family room.
The storm doors are clean and clear as the moment before you hit, breaking the surface neatly
like a diver. It's almost funny—your face, the surprise. Did we start to laugh? Then I'm thinking
not water glass. Glass water. She's just shaking off glass water from glass arms, glass hair.

Sweet sixteen and I dream water turns to glass inside me.

Now I carry glass coins in a glass pocket, think nothing of the crystaled kiss of ice cubes.

At the hospital I hear *severe condition, severed artery.* I think I'll tell you the difference between severe and sever is one thin letter and a vowel besides.

It's been a month. Our birthday today. There is no cake. I buy us a glass balloon, heart-shaped with an echo inside.

HEART PINE*

I was raised in checkered silence.

—Anna Akhmatova

She was diminished through patternless noise
of a lukewarm reststop in an ancient pre history.
Animal silence numbed her.
It was airlessness whose quiet she missed.
She avoided fallow and barren meadows,
most loathsome was the tarnished marshland,
a never-there scarecrow outside of time
whose grinning limblessness
paralyzed her rest with real.
Normally, she perished them.
In her, one tree remains. Then same stumps
against common unspeakings swallow back
above other soil.
She isn't loud—as though a sister survived.

*Written in loose antonymic from English to English from Anna Akhmatova's poem: "Willow."

THIRST

If you ask what's become of me
I have to point to a stranger
on the street and say if there's a prayer left
inside that body
it's blue-skinned and shaky
dog-eared and barely breathing.

If there's a way out, make it magenta
and shrill, tearing at the upholstery.

At night when the trees are mascara
sketches against the weeping sky
I fingerpaint on a rented wall.

And you, I know what you mean.
Every old-time barbershop wounds me,
the pole's warped twisting,
the red stripe that never escapes,
the invisible knife, a spiral of apple skin
falling away and away.

a name filled with ringing
trill's end and undoing

a squiggled thrill unclothed
queen and widow saint of the adopted

the curved boomerang's oath
bring back is possible in myth

Gepetto was never such a greedy God.
You had some autonomy
even though the strings
must've been a drag, Wooden Boy.

This voice is on loan.
Borrowed.
But think about it,
aren't they all?

The hand in my back is one thing
but his words down my throat?

He gave you things:
hinged elbows,
and jointed knees,
a way to measure
the truths a body knows.

of a journey peopled with ever-strangers.

Melting Woman seeks Coldest Man for structure.

Tell me a romance, Mr. Jones.

How light weighs on the weary.

If you don't play the fiddle or a mean banjo strike a triangle to call me in.

Or hum the last bar
of Melancholy Baby and I'm aswoon.

Woozy Girl seeks Dizzy Boy for possible carousal.

Merry-go-round a mulberry bush. A carousel full of berry-drunk ponies
        bellied to spooky music. A world round as a dinnerplate.
        Glee me now.

Let's build a gingerbread house
        on softest frosting snow with spun-sugar windows
        that sweet-cut when they shatter.

Let's never be dead.

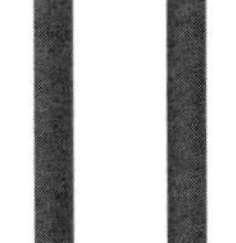

This version contains a body.
The dead sister
life, the daughter, the house

built from shade and light.
The floor aswim with swordfish,
almonds and the catscradle

weave of branches.
Tree arms drip bracelets
of fish shadow and knife.

Place the story otherwise:
the ballroom carpet gone Persian
rug patching the princely floor.

Glass slippers become barefeet
cut to ribbons and the ribbons
of the midnight gown are draperies.

The sad hue of the choked-up sky
gone sadhu with a small lamp
to bear. The carriage a ricksaw

the horses Arabian. The night stitched
to the dry sockets of hurt clouds.
Once castle now oubliette.

Dancer to dungeon and she
rolls into herself. Cloud to cloud
from the sky blue taffeta of sky no less.

Darkening. Night pocketing
the timepiece of the moon.
She keeps the change

hidden from view. In the corners
a ghost-twin waits like the tumbleweed
of cat-fur that bobs through the rooms.

She sweeps it away.
She pulls her name from ashes.
She buries the remains.

ABOUT THE OTHER ANIMALS

The ones Noah forgot, those poor swimmers.
God-fearing ghosts on three legs left sinking
in their own faithless tides. The lungfish
were the last to go. Winded from the flood,
breathless from gossip of someday oil spills,
underwater politics, the coming world; tired
of the swim, they made it to the ark,
to its crowded on-board aquarium just in time.
But the others were denied their passage,
littering the shore like so many
Penelopes and Ariadnes.
I'll return for you, Noah told them,
Wait there on the other bank, I'll be back.

Noah of the nameless wife, who could believe him?
But they did, and they waited. Waited
until their coats grew matted and frayed, until
the sea became all, overpowering, supreme:
water floor, water ceiling, water walls.
Until their lungs deluged, burst open, collapsed.
And Noah? He was just another hero afloat,
an almost-saint with places to go.

(Some say they were the loveliest
of animals. With silvery-scaled
feathers or leopard-spotted fins, toadish pelts,
snowy-furred horns, carapace underbellies, dotted-swiss gills,
phosphorescent dew claws, pure
ivory lashes around jeweled azure eyes.)

Others claim the beasts were to blame
too gracious, too leisurely. Taking their sweet time
and drinking iced coffees with the angels,
reciting poems to the stately gazelles
(who left rudely at Noah's first trumpeting call).
These refined beasts were in no hurry to catch the fleeing ark.
The lost creatures denied
their passage. Always other, always animal.

You can wait, Noah said.
So they did. Swallowed by the storm, suppose
they saw grand things—the throat of the seas,
the underside of an old world and more.
Still, they were left behind.
Rumor has it seven mosquitoes boarded that day,
uninvited, no less; while the other animals
drank the ocean, all seven seas, bits of sky,
maybe more. Call it hearsay, unwritten
history, a last wish, a lie.
That story went down with the old sins
and the olive tree (minus one branch, one dove).
How does it matter now? So many wives'
tales later, rotten apples, borrowed
ribs, snakes in trees, gaps
in the telling and retelling
and untelling.

That story went down.
The world washed clean
and the spaces in the scenery
where they might've stood,
hardly look empty anymore.

She was cider vinegar and cool design
        a whole lot of chrome.
Say I kissed her and that kiss
        brought her back to life;
back to the palace where panacea
        becomes pain again,
cast from rest to royalty,
        corded off in velvet
red. I mean we were finished then.
        Consider it: the spinning wheel
the sleeping she and me there
        waiting   trying to help her rise.
There was nowhere to go in that scene
        (so much asleep between us)
we polished off a whole life in that kiss
        we were nowhere-headed fast fast
in a carriage too pretty to drive.

in a thin gown, thin blooded, thin hearted,
light-headed as a loon and forlorn, too.
Pale moon off a pale moon you parted
these waters once. Too dear to hold, you
sank *Belief*—the only boat to buoy
us. You, Lover whose name is a village
spilling voices in my head. Moody Boy,
you are the whole town—home, steeple and ledge
where I—shrill tragic bird with my trembly
songs fly off, to swoop or to plummet.
Once, I, a maid at your window to be
your Valentine, waited for the pale melt
of your gaze. Now, what swirls in my Gone-Girl head
are three words: *good as dead, good as dead.*

BODIES THAT HOLD US

I was young when you found me, not exactly a saucer
but nowhere near the platter I've become.
There was one night, all that spinning
the spiced rum, the drunken bovine,
the gleeful dog, the musical cat.
You were there too, calling to me
like a picnic, a warm, sudsy bath.
You were there, shiny as a knife
in the moonlight.
And I...what could I do
but run with you?

O Spoon, we had big plans: Venice, Vienna, Venus.
We eloped, slipped into a cutlery
and fine china shipment bound for Italy,
got ourselves little jobs in a waterside cafe.
It was heaven for a while.
So many bowls and forks tried to come between us
but we held strong, Old Spoon.

These days there's so much crazing on my face,
I tell you I fired with crackling glaze.
And you are bent in some weird angle,
nothing, everything as I remember you.
But Spoon, I'd know you anywhere.
We never made it to Austria, found ourselves everywhere
from second-hand stores to greasy (I won't say it) diners.
They're still singing about us, Spoon.

One night sometimes, that's all it takes to make a life
worth it, one good one, most folks can't even claim that.

We had ours, a checkered tablecloth
still spread after a lawn party
under that perfect star-flecked sky,
rum left under a tree where some kids sneaked it away.
The cat serenading us like no gondolier ever could,
sparks flying from the fiddle, whiskers ablaze.
The tipsy dog, beside himself with laughter
and the cow skipping the arc of that grin-crescent moon
as if a jumprope, as if she could be all the sheep
we number on nights when our breath makes us weary,
our bodies worry us, and we are trying desperately
just to fall asleep.

1

*When Lot's wife looked over her shoulder, she turned into a pillar of salt. Pillars hold things up, and salt keeps things clean, but it's a poor exchange for losing your self. People do go back, but they don't survive, because two realities are claiming them at the same time. ***

2

Time: Twilight. On the bank of the Great Salt Lake, a spider weaves a web between two thin reeds, precarious home and so gorgeous. She believed in spider love then, in knitting the selves together—all sixteen legs—a macramé of *closer.*

3

A macramé of closer, the weave of hammock they hung from a knife moon and swung there, in the spoonly afterglow. This was before the Manhattan apartment and long distances, before telephone lines crackled with tumbling buildings, and the murky view in memory from *Windows on the World.* Two summers before catastrophe, they met at such altitude to see what they could salvage. They needed distance, space, a birdseye view. They needed, in a word, *elevation.*

The day was overcast, a bowl of grey broth, and she had to take it on faith that the Hudson shimmered a mile beneath them.

4

A mile beneath them, a man and a woman carried a plethora of helium balloons, explosively bright in the flat bullion light.

5

In the flat bullion light, the subway doors open to a dark river of bodies. Moody beauty's the rage—somber fabric—temperamental skies caught between heartless skyscrapers that scrape the blue and never kiss it better. Implicit sophistication: black coffee, black clothes, clove cigarettes, dressing as a bruise for Halloween, then forgetting to change. She's thirty-four and she misses obvious beauty—sloppy, unrestrained color: yellow, orange, slap-happy pink.

6

Pink burning. To find the body's interior isn't vital rose like a thick wine, but dim as an abandoned mine. Now the window, that table, building, the dinnerplates, the hostess, the afternoon, all lie shattered in a heap of odorous loss. She sees it on the t.v. 1019 miles away.

7

Miles away, water for bones, she craves confluence, a city riding on crossed waters. To eschew stormclouds, never resist bliss be-decked and buoyantly, boisterously so. How far, how fast would she go for obvious joy? In the cliché heartbeat, a blinked eye, in a flash so swift, it fades before she can sew herself in it. In a Houston hour, a San Francisco second, in a

8

*New York, city of motion, could not go forward, and so, because it hated to stand still, it went backwards. Went backwards into its past, individual and collective.**

9

Into its past, individual and collective, the city stretches. Collective noun: A confusion of amnesiacs. A confluence of floating cities. A phase of regrets. Column of sodium loss: no way of getting to where she was.

10

The radio mumbles and mumbles. Salted fields and so many missings.
She was in a phrase,
looking back.

*Text by Jeanette Winterson

· 44 ·

· 45 ·

Love, Girl is what makes the whirls
go round & lunacy ravings swirl
in a smitten girl's moth-eaten soul.
Never you mind them. Those fickle ole
lanternfish boys. All lit up, sure they is.
But all wet. Attract you with slimy fish
lamp bodies. Pretty soon your spirit's soggy,
all dragged down, skinned & boned. Even Hamlet.
Not mean, just wishier & washier
than a moon-eyed girl like you needs. Dance with us,
Miss Ophelia. The strobe lights slow everything
down. The mirror ball turns your face
into a thousand little pictures,
(you see you the way a spider would)
twirling & all broke up. You don't even
have to know just which one you are.

I'M THE MIMI

John F. Kennedy's intern admitted to The Daily News yesterday: "I am the Mimi," Marion (Mimi) Fahnestock, now 60,

called it a huge weight off her shoulders to finally admit her affair with the dashing young President four decades ago.

Forty years of silence, then one whisper to the media & you're out

like an activist, a boxer, a match. Your name

waits with an article hung before it in a muffled murmur, something fish

or divers mouth as they pass. The gossip trafficked in the loud quiet secret

of oceans. The rings lost every year by honeymooners: hard halos fish sometimes

swallow—intrigued by the cold gleam (like your secret) *I'm the Mimi*

a phrase that sounds funny—maybe it's the me

falling over itself, all those ricochet words seem to always go out

wearing silly hats, doubled and yet halved somehow,

and quiet as the years that took that girl with the name

that should have meant more of a self, a double-self, whose steamiest secret

seems almost funny now. Oh Mimi, you wanted them to fish

for a history, shocking as the moment forty years ago that reporters called *fishy*

as they approached the car and you were the young head bobbing in his lap, Mimi.

They said they first thought you a Kennedy child, then they understood & kept the secret

that, in a way, you sort of were. Nineteen, & flying about

in a plane equipped with his every comfort, your name

on that list of things to pack for him, his down time, good time

girl. The quiet ink of your job description: "presidential sexual release" sometimes

whispered in the offices where these things get written the way fish

write underwater with a curve of the spine, bodies bent in a bluish dream. The name

you were called by a lover who never knew Marion, the mother, the wife. Only Mimi:

a forever-girl to him when he died. Newly wed, you'd been out

of his life only two months, dodging guesses and the trouble they'd secrete.

Valentino: that lipreader's valentine understood about secrets,
died with his own in a New York hospital, alone & full of the quiet that sometimes
follows when you lie about what you love. When your heart goes out
to the world and your mouth moves soundlessly as fish
mouth o in hunger, in sickness, in vain. Damn old then, where wherever you go, Mimi
becomes a vanishing point. You want your daughters at least to know your names

all starring in the real movie of your life which is no silent film with a star whose name
rings with love voicelessly scripted on the screen. One future self a forever-kept secret:
So much was trying to quiet me. But from that ragdoll quiet, You'll be The Mimi
once again, your lips stitched long-enough with threads and threats of times,
selves nearly forgotten. (Has it been forty-one years?) It's mid-May, you lie in bed fish-
mute for the last night, thinking of your girls & tomorrow's news when the story's out.

Sometime, under-glass-quiet, a fish full of wedding bands sashays by. Another day blows out.
Each lover re-names us in a way. *This me*
or that, Daughters, try to understand, I didn't want to die, sinking with my own shiny secrets.

BOYCOTTING THE PLANETARIUM

Given Venus, given rooms of relentless
bedtimes, heavens fake as heavenness, stars un-
plugged at closing time, and given the sprayed-on
    comet, a falling

star that falls and stays on fallen: forget the
dreaming husbands, school-kids, wanderers, boy scouts
—also the armchair astronauts hiding
    out from every

other sky, the cruel eclipse and the always-
same casino light. I feel you, all cashed-
out on supernova remnants and
    overdrawn in space,

hating every planet, each bit of take-back sky.
No, not my idea of a galaxy: inside-
out and flat of face: can't sparkle, can't see even
    to see, My Dear.

Tell that mean-sad zodiac (tell your-
self, too) strike this here aphelion year, its
deep-turned-cold time and frayed denim overhead,
    all of the tin-alone.

Lose the red shift, ring me up some bit of stellar
something. Give me a spitwad, boomerang moon and
constellation-silly-strings, the gorgeous,
    awful all of it.

and even harder to stay. What with its real
trees and real leaves and real loves and real leaves
and that it doesn't take sci-fi to turn it all alien.

I'm a fan of the tangible, the slow-cooked oatmeal,
the dying pigeon crouched by the base of the tree,
the velour of baby hair against the hand. Pomegranates:

the ruby tears dressed in their transparent rain-jackets.
And why can't moments be labeled as they happen?
HERE COMES HIS LAST WORD. THIS IS ABOUT TO BE YOUR LAST TOUCH.

So no miracle's ever lost, like that day when the taxi
collects us from the movies and we skittle home in the rain
make dinner, believe, love and then call it, (how-could-we?) a day.

Later that same summer, someone pulls away
from the curb saying *gone*, saying *for good*.
The morning is an over-full clothes hamper. We miss so much.

And when he shall die, take him out the ballgame
and bat around a little eternity with his wooden leg.

Cut him out in little stars and sew them
on the majorette's epaulets, let him
serve himself up like a galaxy.

He will make the face that says icky
so tell him *Heaven-so-fine go fetch me some soap*
and he will because he loves when we call him

anything that sounds a little infinite. All the world
loves a sorry knight. He's a simile
for nothing. Pay no worship

to the garish one. He's a soluble prince in a lather
of time. He's the plan
with the built-in roaming fee.

Don't expect him to come through
the bad weathers. Don't ask him to
do anything that rhymes with shower or glove.

Accept the things he's best at doing instead:
salting fields, playing dead.

WISHING BONE SPELL TO END EMPTINESS AT TWILIGHT OR THE BED'S EXPANSE OR RAGE AT A CLOUD SHAPED LIKE THE TRUNK OF A MUSCULAR MAN

The wishing bone of a human lover

You must find the first lost beloved

Sacrum: A triangular bone shaped like a splayed jellyfish

You must wear the musk of grieving beast

Just before the tailbone built into the spine and wedged there

Your own rancid sorrow will do

It floats inside the pelvic ring

Go to the house of your first heart

Its motion is passive

Run a blade along the lines of his spine

Both keystone and foundation to the spinal column

Use the tip of the knife   You must open him

It is for walking

Unlock this bone wing remove it

The weight-bearer

Cleanse it with water and sun

Arched between two innominate bones

For three thrice-lived days

The point in the body where two opposite forces

You may make an amulet if he loved the most

Upper and lower body meet in a common focus

wear it as a charm to recall his charms

It is indeed one inch behind the centre of gravity

If you loved more find a stone bowl

The wishing bone of a human lover

and a pestle grind it down to finest bonemeal

Sacral Of or near the sacrum

season everything you eat with it for nine days

Sacral A half-sacred place to be

The flavor may recall the lover flightless
Floating in the pelvis encircled in desire
Weep at the dry taste the familiar ache
Built into the spine and wedged there

There is a sky like no sky
I've ever seen before and I want to
        hunker down in it.

    We were caught between
a hurricane and what-happens-next.

Our modus operandi was Hoping for the Best.
Our weapon of choice: Departure.
Our favorite dancestep: The Wishy-Washy,
we dipped and called that motion: The Globe Indelible
if only we'd known, if only we'd known.

Certain spells light a tulip of flame on a bare palm,
others send two doves back into the dark tunnel
of coat sleeve. You, a wool blazer with a silk-lining
stitched stunning from another time,
knew how to use magic as a verb
and lasso the wildebeests, so we slid into a magnetic
poem and stayed awhile. The honeymoon stanza
was plush, our credit cards beyond the limit, you planted
a prism of peppers, praised my heliotropic face,
plucked spiderlilies in my honor, called a rainbow collect
then reversed charges to my front yard so that I had paved road
to my own patch of heaven. That many colored beanstalk
and you Jack, were the only gentle-eyed gardener in town
who could whip a giant's ass and a tomato basil soufflé
all in the same afternoon.

One August, a troop of frogs popcorned the forest floor
and the rain polka-ed across the ballroom lake.
We were newly concatenated and five seasons
had yet to have their way with us.

        We fell open
like a jewelry box, everything sparkley
spilling out and no chimey music, no plastic ballerina
twirling on a single screw in a tutu made of stiff cheesecloth
or some sorry excuse for the kind of net that could catch
anything and keep it for long.
        Save history and words—which will hold us
pieta-ed—in the glare off their plate-glassed face
with a view.   Whenever I say Darling,   I'll always mean you.

We were cashed out so you found pennies, saved crickets,
Sold the oil-spill casing of the june bug for kisses.
I mis-sent letters, I made afraid. If there was a dimmer switch
in that bright season, I was the one who found it.
The sky went tornado-y and we looked for cover
under the wide-open very-heaven
and you palimpsested a forever
into that liveable-fall of an afternoon.

We made elevators and ferris wheels into the saddest inventions.
(Anything that tried to lift us up, held us down.
Kept everyone's tongues in their own seamless mouths.)
        We missed the fair (everything sounding metaphorical now)
stayed too long in a town whose nearest amusement
park was four hours away.

We magiced the dim, bicycled out into
a noon foggy with mosquitoes.
        You were so sorry then, never knowing how loved you were
for your foolish plans your worldwide open heart. I'm beachbound

        to climb that lifeguard chair and from such a height,
to say: You luster the seashells: abalone in and stay for a while, won't you,
my wife of a flooded kitchen with ghost utensils swimming
free of the black linoleum. Let me cover you in seashell armor:
the broken terrapin (the same autumn green that pools inside
your eyes), our only blues stolen from the rescued-crustaceans
of your childhood, some mother-of-pearl for moping. We were hoping
for a break in the storm, a change of weather
a train that sews us stitch by iron stitch
to a town not at all this town. We despised the wandering minstrels
except for the boy who did wheelies, and the one who stayed home,
a boy with haystack hair and an angelic elf who flew
from his heels when he sang:
        they were our own.

You were the boy who saw faces in bark and the knotholes
of every living tree. Who saw something in me
(so I blinded him). I won't let it be true
that I've forgotten how to kiss you.

You well-meaner, joy generator, you splint
the giraffe's crooked neck with the last popsicle stick
cross of the yard sale. You balsa-wood pilot
in love with flight. Your name begins
with a three-step ladder
I've spent centuries, Darling, trying to climb.
Now I'm left to this sign language:
take care, I spell you, take care
in a knapsack slung over your shoulder
if anyone asks say I gave you all I had
if anyone asks say it was I who put it there.

You caller in of rainbows, hair wild as you are
tender at the eyes—never mind touch
just to look at you is so much. This is a morning song for lovers'

yoohooing back over the wide distance of the day ahead.
Oh savior of the box turtle, the struck squirrel, Ben Franklin
of the box kite, this is a mourning song
full of piccolos and strung to a housekey worn
down from five seasons
of who we were and how we loved and tied to the kite
that sewed a boy like you to me and drew,
(still draws) an etch-a-sketch of electricity.

PIÑATA GROVE

*Then I would come at once my love with love Bringing to wasted areas the sight
of butterfly and swan and turtle dove*
—Eavan Boland

I should make coffee, make do
with what's left of the night,

and stop thinking about those baby frogs
popcorning the forest floor
so that each step we took
started a kind of polka
dance-hall of bodies, frantic
to the beat of our big human feet
on the late summer ground.

I confuse that day with pecan picking
and the way you'd javelin
the broom handle into the charted sky
until pecan rain surrounded us
and we followed that brindled falling
knowing that later would mean pie.

Tonight there'll be no relief
map marking every polka-dotted
trail we ever walked, every storm
we weathered, and what's left is the nature
channel where even the wolverine's fierce love
has to hold tenderness, where even the weather's at a loss.

Am I to make of these images some kind of design
pointed and sharp as the teeth of some predator?
Why take all this terror to make us run
back for what we love?

Always, in the Serengeti of a moment: a gazelle, her young,
the threat of some wordless okay from the grasses sssslhlhh
danger that whispery strikes fast
        as a mama gazelle charges in,
and the snowglobe of who we were turns
        upside down, so that even false
blizzards, even frogs fall up
in a season that, like the logic of love, defies gravity,
sputters out a curtain of moving Braille that if we could make it out
would say nothing less than this:
        I would come at once my love, my love,
wear the cruel lightning of their jaws as a necklace.

You were taking an ordinary breath when the whole ocean made twin mothwing pools of your lungs, when they took you in your wet suit and hung you out to dry.

I wanted to know what the ocean floor knew of you. *Last kiss. Open-mouth. Sea in. Brother gone.* I wanted to see God there: enormous, gathering you like branch coral—years in the delicate growth and then broken off like the needliest icicle, like glass cello strings. Something you'd take when reaching for something else. An extra newspaper. A hotel shower-cap. You might have been an accidental looting.

God there wearing you like a pendant—He that large and you my heart-shaped muscle of sibling reduced to a pendant really, a single charm hooked on the chain of his neck fluttering when he took a breath, caught against his pulse, against the light. Yes, wrong to it. Wrong as only a big boy with a John Wayne swagger heart-throbbing the neighborhood can be, folded in on himself like an origami crane caught in the rain.

In your honor, we will plant a Japanese elm this summer when the heat makes any labor passion. I cut a lock of hair to bury where you are. I will send the large round garden stone you befriended to a land so cold it will crack it open and in the center will be a single drop of saltwater—that's how I'll know you now.

for Wallace

Here it is. The dark forest we never had to visit, having done time
    there in our hearts. Yes, *all is silver*, it is.

Tonight a friend told me: *this weather—the temperature of dreams.*
    He means no temperature, the way fish wouldn't understand wetness.

All *is* silver: the tarnished Black Sea, the Romanian woman fifty years beyond
    the sinking ship that drowned her young man. *You see, so old*, she tells me, *I never marry.*

Even this thick Southern air—*silver* and the tin heart we brought back all the way
    from Mexico to a home I would leave behind, dissolve into this nothing-climate,
    a thin night, so little to keep it all together. Too much history empties a place.

·

Some nights I imagine for them: his return, ragged from sea-time but whole. The fewest words
and his voice rasped but the woman has held it in the bones of her skull and remembers for
him. In the bed that waited silent-years for him, they retire and his sounds there are enormous,
the woman sure he can be heard from Bucharest to Baia Mare, every streber, every sterlet in
the Danube wide-awake now, but it is his touch, the finger pads that speak songs straight into
her veins that the woman will replay. In the morning as she dresses, she'll smile at the wall
where she believes his cries have left echoes and residual aftershocks rippling sound waves deep
through the plaster. No, let's say the walls are stone, and each mineral recalls one note so that
the score of his return is composed in the core of each rock.

·

The nickel key ring given as a promise left rust stains on my finger. *Coat it with something real,*
we told the jeweler, *platinum, white gold, even silver.* Nothing would stick. Sometimes, for just a
minute I want to be back there, walking the corner that elbowed from my street to his,

and feeling that dry pain again. I moved away to a town rendered in oil paint, nothing dries
without curling up or rotting. The buildings smell of mildew in summer when the sky is a grey
satin hammock, a swollen crescent hanging low with the burden of rain, though nothing so

rich as that heartbreaking color of twilight, the heaviness-suffering-lavender-light. I want
to be back there for just a minute, years before I'd been acquainted with this present life: new,
moist, giving and withholding. A life where what you love either moves ahead of you at a set
distance like painted anguished steeds on a carousel impaled in place or it trails behind you fifty
paces or so

and you use every reflective thing you have to catch a glimpse of it: the plate glass of the dry
cleaners, in the plexiglass of the bus-stop and what you see when you see anything is yourself
there, milling behind, trying hard not to catch up with you.

•

Cold, dark, deep, absolutely clear, element bearable to no mortal, our English teacher read aloud,
then told us a story about coming out of surgery dazed and irritable to her husband there
hovering over her. She asked him to go home and he did or he tried,
until the accident pinned him in a web of sirens and red, frantic light.

The last time I ever spoke to him, she told us, *and I did it all wrong.*
Now I tell people how I feel before I walk out of a room, before I roll over to sleep.
If you don't remember anything else from seventh grade: take this down; commit it to memory.

I believed, grew up to tell too much for fear I'd never get the chance.
        Here's the real sadness: no one cares to know.

•

This weather—dreamy absence—it reminds me, the easy arousal of certain saxophone music, a
deep, low richness, or the violin's complicated bliss, horsehair to strings, the sweet

scratch of cricket legs, implicit polish, troubled shimmer: (*I want you,*) or I did, once.
        Then I meant to say something else about deep blue or black

swans (they mate for life). I meant to talk about smoke and brass and burning.
There was more to say about dusk: (west of us still) in a purple so blue it breaks your heart.

I meant to mention the way your left arm swings out when you walk and slices the horizon
        into strange diagonals. The minor miracle of earlobes, the sheen of foil-light on

the wet street some Tuesday when I hoped you saw how sterling an afternoon
        could be. The forgiveness
of the seasons, the rebate of leaves upon the trees.

•

When we dream we dream of lost things: a dead lover, an engagement ring worn
            on a chain around the neck for more than fifty years.

I will always want to know you the endless circle was meant to mean.
            I know what you mean: willed-tarnish and forever.

Yes, all is silver, but it's old silver. You will die, that's all
            and I won't know, or I will, and you won't know that I knew.

One way or another we're going down. In light of that, bring me good coffee, a red paper
        parasol, whatever you're reading right now, your voice and your hands.

My Romanian pen pal is seventy-three, and she says she still braids questions
into her prayers for her drowned man: *What did you mean by dying?*
                            Mute, unrelenting, you made the quietest love.

LAST WISH FOR THE DOLLMAKER'S GHOST

If there is only one world let it rise
flambeau-style on a black & silver '84 Virago
hopelessly late and not a bit sorry.

Let it call to women who are kindling
for the slow stare of one poet
late to his own blessing.

If there is only one world let it fall
to its knees, jazz after the bars close,
blast down Second South reckless & restless

full of good intentions
just one more time for the sake of the wistful.
Let it hold a hundred strangers,

misty over Keats in a late afternoon
class with leaf shadows casting knives through a west
window & breaking a shy woman's heart

in the back row. He was on his way
to everywhere. Of course, he was stopped at the border.
Those mountains thought they had him, thought he'd roll

from one lip of that drunken town to the next,
thought he couldn't hear those sad sax cries, blue notes:
You're my thrill but he knew better so

he wandered, dipped into a white sky, breathed
angels & fire, downed straight shots of sorrow,
kissed that strange salted valley good-bye

& sped to a city that celebrates defeat.
Finally his papery heart gave in
imploded origami, a failure

of percussion, a final sweep of syllables
& freest verse. *It is late for blessings
but go on, bless everything a little.*

If there is just one world, it is wan & wanting
& for some reason, it mattered once.

TEARING AWAY

The pain of life overrides the joy to the point that joy does not exist.

—Kevin Carter, a photojournalist and Pulitzer Prize recipient for the photograph of a starving Sudanese child crawling
to a feed station while a vulture waited over her body. Sixteen months after taking the photo Carter committed suicide.

You must've wondered if Abraham's hand was shaking too, believing
he'd sacrifice his son.
You would've thought it a simple task since God was bound to step in
and stop that hand.
      That day, your camera, your hands, could you have stayed them?
But it was just the three
of you then: the child, the scavenger and you.
If the angel of God was in Sudan that day,
        you missed the shot.

Some say it's hard to tell which is the vulture.
Squatting as you were and waiting, the shadows must've been similar.
You waited a long time for that bird to spread its wings
and when it didn't, you captured it this way: wings down,
a cloak of a body, a black spade, a caped heart, looming
and already looking a little smug.
And the child, a sun-baked clothespin doll whimpered,
while you waited, her body, by now, a dry sculpture
of mud and twigs, a jungle gym grid
of bones crouched on the dirt and grass so scorched it was straw.
      Some used to say if anyone could turn straw to gold it was you. If they wondered how
you could bear the body defeated, the unnatural hunch of the spine, they didn't say. It must've
been a long afternoon, the nature of the terrain, the slow sun, a lazy-plumed hunter, the girl and
you. How could you know a child so small could weigh so much?

      All we knew of Africa were images, visual puzzles always missing pieces. We were too
young to absorb much, American girls prone to spells and trances. We'd remember little
beyond the hot dry air and the bright beads
we traded among ourselves.

We didn't even know an impala from a gazelle.
But we loved the magic woman, her warm cocoa skin,
her ears stretched so long with heavy hoops,
the hole made it easy to see through to the other side.
She would tell us—three sisters—
     When a man gives you a flower
whose color grows brighter after it dries up and dies, this man loves you with such power, that his life
is yours. And we were transfixed, all three of us, enchanted, our breath held.

Back in the states we saved each flower
for years after proms and valentines had passed.
     Then it happened, I loved a man whose red rose grew unbearably bright, not the dried
blood scab-red of others but a fearful scarlet. I wanted to show my sisters,
     find the magic woman again, but even before the rose died, the man was already gone.
     Enough happens and you stop believing. Africa becomes words, savage, primitive, painted
faces, and tribal dances, in National Geographic. Suffering becomes souvenir. We never see our
own faces stamped on ghost beads: astonished, a frozen scream. Not our hunger
bathed in sweat
     primal and dark.

I had to think visually. You said. *Dead guy, splash of red, blood on sand. Like that. But inside,* you
said, *inside you scream Oh, God.*

The bird, you, Abraham. All posed and ready. But nothing stops the sound of the child for you,
hands over your ears, pillow over your head, where the sound is a high-pitched bell wailing.
(Though that day, while you waited, it had been faint, barely heard.) Sometimes you think you
filled the sound in later, she was far too weak and memory just lent her a voice. Your friends
said it was symptom of all the drugs: ringing of the ears. But you knew better.

What about Isaac, could he forget the picture
of his father above him, the knife, the terrible moment between
the light off the blade and God's voice?
What burns one image in, leaves a brand on the tissue of memory
so that the leap from here to forgetting is wider,
more treacherous than all of Serengeti in the rainy season?

At times you'd recall how you loved Mozambican prawns,
the call of hyenas, the perilous stillness
of early morning on the plains.
Some say you were grieving
for the film you'd lost
or the shots missed by a split- second.
As if there weren't enough pictures,
you smoked the white pipe: dagga weed and tranquilizer.
If there was something in that smoke
which simplified Africa
you never found it.

Maybe you told the critics I take pictures not lives
or the readers of Time magazine
who wanted to adopt that very child
that child, the one in the photo
that there were more, whole galleries of them,
if they were interested. Of course, they weren't.
They say you saw terrible things: a group of men shot
and falling dead into a car. (Later you'd say you missed this shot,
pushing the button a millisecond
        after the gun fired.)
This was all months before you would fill your car with carbon monoxide, sit in the driver's seat
and wait.
        By then it was May.

On the seat next to you the note:
        Not *the lost photographs that finally did it, but the pictures I could not remove.*

Not *haunted, wounded, killings, corpses, famine.* Not *trigger-happy madmen, birds of prey.*
Just *cease-fire and nightmare and done.*

NOTES FOR HOW TO CARRY THE MEMORY OF THE BODY

Across this threshold, stupid as war, across the statelines
the uncut ribbons between us. Lift me as you would a fingerprint

then wipe the surface of your life shiny again. Recall me as one
who meant to strip down the nightsky for you. Recall the rain

and the art building balcony, the storm whipped into something
that the trees and I never forget. So lay me down like an over-read letter

or let the machine pick me up. There's a million windows for leaving
this room but the way back is

The sky's all dimey, the moon bizarre and tomorrow still
a touch to the left of anywhere   (your touch remains

all). I meant to ghost you like the tannic galaxy of fallen leaves
the sidewalk spoked like stars, like infant handprints

grappling with the concrete. Dried and not dead satellites
off something so brightalively as you. I never want to see you

sad again or haunted by the bare trees where once we shook pecans
out of the sky. Let's recall what fell there and what sweetness you spun it into.

The leopard-hide shade that turned us into the kind of cats
that could've hung in such a climate, such a season, with so much danger

we stalk back, show our teeth and do not lay down like dumb beasts
slow beasts, craving our own demise.

I'll recall that only you, only you

        Hush Love, the only the thing that matters is what takes us down
into sleep and who, each day, revives us and if there is something off

to that pear-slice moon hung there tonight, keep walking;
from such a distance, to try to put a finger on it, means you blot it out.

I take it back,
he was rotting from the day you met him:
making himself known first
by the dull ache he left in your spine.
(This should've told you something, Princess.)

Outside the tower, twenty mattresses down we saw him foul and spoiled. Outside the palace
gates we have known him, waited for the steady throb of your back to tell you, Princess. What
begins with pain leaves a kind of soreness, hard to forgive.

Somewhere a fairy godmother embroiders white eyelet trousseau pillows: *What tries, strengthens.*
No matter how many times you come around this will always be your story, Princess, and the
only laws laid down will be your own.

Before the wedding the seamstress
tells you the kingdom gossip:
how your groom watched you
from a distance, breathed in your beauty,
squeezed all the fruits at the open-air market
while you, fresh, sweet, unhandled,
one stand away,
asked the florist for lilies.

By now your dress has dragged on dirty steps, caught in at least one carriage door, your train
tripped you on the way down the aisle, sent you falling into him.

Three toasters later, two electric can openers, five crockpots, one torn veil, he takes you, wipes
out the only memories you have of the circular room in a locked tower, the quiet nights, the

sometimes dreams that kept you going. He scrubs them away with the scouring pad of his voice, the harshness of his hands.

Those will be the strains you remember
no music, just the small prince inside you
heel against your backbone,
his charge to daylight
pushing out, the pull again
when you hold him over one hip.
The new weight of your breasts
swollen with milk, tugging
at your back reminds you
of that first night, twenty beds deep,
the thin blood from that elevation,
the dent in your spinal column,
the soft pain that never subsides.

You know it's a long fall down
when you dream from such an altitude,
when the body beside you lies
in the deepest of darkness,
but you believe what they've told you
that what shapes a princess
keeps her up all night
rests hard on her bones
takes her down from a high place,
takes her down to size.
They've told you what forms a princess,
bruises her, spells its name
with a hard caress in the small
of her back.

Unless. There was an owl down on the banks of a certain river.
All summer it decayed, all but that curious call. All who listened
mistook it for the organ music of mystery radio dramas. They woke
briefly and then turned to their living. All summer it spoke,
and from where they stood —the boy, the girl who had seen
its breathing, the hushed rise where it once lifted soundlessly,
now perceptible and laborious, as if flight were a hoisting of the dead weight
of one body exerted by a tired body —it seemed terribly unreal.
The girl had thrown the rock partially just to make it real.
The girl had thrown the rock hard and the quiet strike, the true damage,
surprised her. She meant to aim well, she had meant, in some other place
and time, to be willing to bring the owl down and her arm remembered
that brutal wish though the girl tried to withdraw the arc of the throw, the trueness.
She felt the rock hit as if it had never left her hand, and her hand felt
the exact cushion of body to stone and the girl would own
that moment for always. Owl body. Stone hand. The owl's grace re-translated
from the floating mass of one language into the heavy Slavic of another.
The owl took forever to die and when it finally did, its accusations sounded
to the girl like hope, and its accusations sounded and sounded for weeks after,
so that the hollow in the middle of some nights shook with that voice.
The river shone messages to the owl in the blinking of several stars
and the boy, a little older now, thought he could decipher the code.
The girl couldn't understand. The owl's cries only sounding like blame to her.
The lights on the river flashed bright with regrets and the boy seemed now
to have turned away from her, so that all she had: the memory of that blow,
she carried alone. What she couldn't forget: the honor of living on the inside
of the boy's life, where he shared what he carried in his pocket with her: the hard candies
swiped from the corner store, the spent shell found outside a robbed bank, the inky
shapes he stamped on his hand, on hers, the minnows that died so that he might

teach the girl to fish. That the boy's face held the regal secrecy, the wisdom
and taloned-cruelty of owls. That what the girl loved so much
and what she took aim at was the same deep-deep-alone in the owl and the boy
who could go well-deep inside himself and leave the girl in the shushed heft
of an owl's intent to fly. That what the girl took aim at and loved so much
was that portable solitude of both boy and owl and the feathery rush
of proximity. That what she loved too, in both, was the rivery reflection
of her own loneliness in them. What the boy couldn't know
was just how she had loved the owl, had waited some nights
alone in the night terror of the forest for the quiet
that could only mean owl's flight. But the boy did know what it meant
to fear what is loved so much that it could take so much less than
a thrown stone or a single killing minute to bring it down.

All's here that was; you know the rest. I keep having that dream though. The twilit one, everything periwinkle and we are waiting at the train station. I somehow sense you are leaving me then though all night you insist you will not. We wait for so long, it becomes waiting and something beyond: that ragged hour too close to morning, we've wrestled too long, the night is sticky, hot air has seeped around us, and we are just trying to grasp the one, final tattered motion that allows for sleep. The night is sticky and what it adheres to is Mexico and our worst hour, so that when the train arrives, you board without me and I keep waiting for you to look back, but you have always walked swiftly, without regrets.

It switches then and we are at the opera, the final act and I haven't the heart even to applaud. I love the Italian, but there have been too many hours spent reading supertitles through blurry eyes. My face a watercolor that doesn't dry. I was six again, my brother's friends came over. Six, a little sister, a tag-along, a pest just wanting to be where they were. *Make like a tree* they'd say *and leaf.*

Tell me now, that history doesn't make a nuisance of its flash-back self. We walk home after rain, you hold my hand absently. I shake branches, send silver-drops-showering-cool upon us. *Pennies from heaven,* I say, *no, dimes from the sky.* You don't laugh anymore and it's no dream now: I know you're leaving. I've always loved the tree-like, the winter-trees: made mostly of shadows and spaces. The old you would make a sexual innuendo. Instead you hold my face in your hands and I want to read something into it but now I brace myself. I say something silly because I know the end of this story, so go ahead, make like a tree.

Back out of this and into a night where
batwings brush the catatonic air.
The road crisps silver in rain's afterglow.
On the third floor balcony, a woman
hangs in a sphere of lantern light reading
the hint of chill in trees about to turn
to stars cut hand-shaped from colored paper.
The trees wear secondhand raincoats whose torn
pockets spill coins from the sky's spare change.
Nothing's desolate in the lampposts or
insects clicking against the light, fireflies
slow in their glowing but the woman tastes
mourning in their cindered wake, the ashes
on their wings, the futile flicker of their ache.

Years after the afternoon in the bears' bungalow, the estranged Goldilocks leaves a
note on her
          husband's pillow.

I was skating on thin ice
                              between who you'd been
                                                          with and where and when
and how I wanted you.

I mean I was skating   on *the* thin ice   and whose name you'd italicized.

The italics a bunch
of noisy neighbors   disturbed

              keeping us awake   leaning into us

Sometimes in an excess
of design they gave us   bold-faced exclamations   accenting each breath:

A boy in this town can translate rain. A girl we know has hung from stars. A horse drowned.
Pity it. A man crossing a bridge on a bicycle rides opposite the river water for eight kilometers.
The day closes in on him. A teaspoon of light runs out. How many sorrows can we cram
in the metal box? If Matilda boards a carousel—say The Bronx Zoo carousel where the
jumping ponies were carved in 1908—long before Matilda was—how many priests would
run bathwater before the music stopped? How many gamblers would run ponies? How many
snowflakes would fall between us? What divisive distance would be just right, Baby Bear? How
cold is the porridge before us. How cold.

Or a blade—a luminous thing.
She is that spider piñata dropping
from the moon on thread the color of water,
of glass dreaming itself
      a rain-beaded curtain.

Half of her wants to woman again,
to tender and to spin, to pocket that worn
coin of moon. Or when slivered,
a shaving of leftover light
she will look to from the window of her
never-again human home.

Now neatly tucked in the corners of the world,
she is so much girl again
bellied against a wall, pulling from inside the knot
& makings of a stringy asylum.

Her mind cocooned in its own sticky threads.
Her love glassed and weaponry,
a shrunken torso and too many spindly vulnerable limbs,
more entangled than tenderness should ever be,
a thousand sorries kept under separate distant beds.
Old apologies knifely as bits of glass
seek the beloved feet and slit the broken
branches of belief.

Still she has been many-armed for so long,
      she holds many spidery loves.

The leaves cut from pumpkin paper and old light.
The tinkling of glass music hitting a water-colored sky.
The tree limbs so intricately woven against midnight
every finger bone wakes to the lacemaker's ache.

Her arms quadrupled and still she can only hold so much
memory, December, prayers:
which are, after all, the glassiest things.

She's come to this:
A papier-mache spider bobbing from a wishful machete moon
slicing through high stringy grasses of rain
growing from the other side of the sky.

Minerva's fury is a javelin of sky-zing & white fire.
Arachne looks to lightening
        needle-blade and promise
to strike her down,   puncture her, and hope what spills
from the split belly of her—an early quiet sky, tuneless,
a cameo face strung on a pocket mirror,
the tapestry lyres unstrung—finally fills her.

BODY GLITTER

The darkness is nothing with prongs. A paradox.
—Aimee Mardin

Light beyond itself. Death standing in a sequin gown flashing brilliance in Morse code to an old woman on a shore three lifetimes back, armed with nothing but a hand mirror.

The woman remembers the girl. A star's age back. And age coming on like cool weather. She thought vertigo and could feel the dizziness of a body weary with gravity. Just a hint: Sahara sands of bewilderment just beginning to whip around her. The sharp kiss sting against her face. She knew it was close. A giant hand willing her to fall back into the palm of confusion.

A star-ago she folded the sky like laundry. Swept up whole seasons in a romantic dustpan. Her hands: dried spiders. Her hair, woven rivergrass. Something about the way skin remembers. Beyond any way back.

Stars lie and spider by. From another world they watch her die. Their telescopes set to nostalgia's forgiving light

Black ribbon. Constellation. Beam her back just one sincere glint. Current. A currency of starlight coins strewn and unspent. Light that knows her time. Her love's name. Lets her ride youth's gorgeous turnstile one more round. Breaks the tallow of her down molecule by molecule. Sculpts her anew from something firmer than soapstone, talc, candlewax.

Matter could matter this universe around. Wind charged with true light. A glassblower's shaping breath. The air unstale, crystalline.

There was something he made you want to say
about light touching water. Ariadne, you hold tight
reins on her desire.
Even when winding twine through the labyrinth
to guide him, I don't think he knew
how you pass time playing strange harps with bird hands.
Chanting, repeating his name to still yourself

Ariadne, I know
about women who fall
for the hero every time.

Theseus, your dark ship.
The power in his voice, the way he shifts
your nightgown.

Sad princess, tired wife, you grew pale
watching waves that might bring him back

When your "hero" didn't claim you
and the island did, Dionysus crowned the night
sky with your tiara.
(Shouldn't hero mean: belief
beyond longing and time?)

Ariadne, you are the one to touch still waters.
To save the men who call themselves heroes.
Shouldn't hero mean: finding your own way back?

Or if at night, he
and your sister curled like spoons
around each other are haunted
by a Cretan princess in a thin nightgown
always facing the sea.

GRETEL AFTER DARK

Night again and a cry
in the dark is the same
cry love teaches us
and we are fluent
in the tongue of need
so the men watch us
like fires and we bend
for them but we don't
burn and we dance
best as cinders a little burnt
ghost little lean-to our bodies
cannot keep our spirits down
we spit ourselves up night
after night but it looks
to anyone like pleasure the lean
in for a whisper and every
man we speak to is someone's
Hansel someone's *only-you-know*
what-it-means-to-be-led-into
the-woods-like-a-stray
and-turned-away-from
(every man's back is a turning
away father, a brother who
says he wasn't there, that he
doesn't even recall the cat
on the roof trying to say goodbye)
we're still trying to say goodbye
here the music starts and we make
of ourselves a slow syrup a melt

the thin sugarglasswindow's nap
on our tongue we slowmelt
into departures we never wanted
at all but they were given to us
like crumpled bills tucked between
our breasts slipped into
our waistbands as if something
of value or intimate in the way
a vanished brother can only be
walking away from a whole
room of sisters each circling
like caged cats each circling
a steel pole like a memory
each memory a pole shot through

a postcard from the pussycat

The boat, is pea-green, sea-green?
I want to tell you everything
since from dry land, you must wonder.
I've taken to the sea in a small boat
of indescribable green with a most elegant bird.
He is all my favorite words: bone and blood and hand.
He reads me stories until my breath runs to a deep purr.
I curl into him fur to feather, plume to paw, talon to claw.
Up all night, we're the perfect pair, I bathe him
with my rough cat-tongue, he teaches me to fly.
Some nights it's enough
to reach over and touch sweet dark resting wings, dreams of flight. We live on honey, mince and
slices of quince which we eat with a runcible spoon. *Which we eat with a runcible spoon.* We're
bound for anywhere, I'll work at a bookstore and the owl, he'll play his small guitar, sing dim
low songs in a cafe by the water.

This side of desire you're forgotten as your phone numbers, your birthdays, your collective pets
and allergies. There on the shore, you are a sorry sight, the mangy lot of you, the lost glance
back. Tonight under such a sky: spread like a suspended tablecloth, shaken out, about to land,
so many stars for silverware,
I am lost to you. I've seen the other side of the seasoned moon, shaken
in the shuddering city. I've wandered the streets, sang slo-berry brandy tunes across rooftops,
stood by blazing trashcans surrounded by rats turning their dirty paws to the flame. I've seen
you: tomcats, alley cats, flea-ridden and cold, seen the needle
in the crook
of your collective arm, the lost things that follow you. I was one, once.
I've heard your scavenger hearts pounding
on the wall outside my lover's room
until he turned that room to the wide open sea

and we let that pulse rock us to sleep.

I've known you, wild dogs, wolverine, wildebeast,

all wrong stops on a pointless journey.

But I am here, against the bluest night sea with the owl and the boat and the full, full moon.

I am drinking in the skyline, I am spooning the water into a cloud and mailing it back for you

and you and all of you.

I can't hear what you most want to say, though that whisper in your throat
just demolished a firefly.

STEPHANIE ROGERS

ETIOLATION

Some rooms you can't find your way out of for years.
—Silvia Curbelo

Two stories up from Virginia Street
in the balmy wind of Alabama
Sexual weather, my friend says
Yes, I allow, *I know this*
but I don't know what to do about it.

If you were here
you'd tell me to keep
the drapes drawn,
you'd look up from the street
each time you passed,
and I'd watch for you.

After so much history
what can we do but look up?
I think I mean second cousin to passion
smokescreens of desire
I think I mean
what you leave is more than residue
cloud chamber tracing
but less than matter,
more than a measure
for disbelievers but let's face it
less than we'd hoped.
I think I mean
more than a cupped hand
could forget about fire
I think I also mean
more than a charred hand

could forget about fire.
Or something about the words I love
icicle minnow linger
the way they hurt a little
laid out that way.

I never told you:
from the third floor
I watched you cross the street
so small I could cover
a whole you with one hand.
From such a distance, you're bearable
a tiny tin soldier I could pick up,
hold in one generous palm.
Or curl my fingers around
make a small dark room,

fling you to the ground
the way my father does
with flies. Their lint bodies
a dull thud on the tile.

Tonight this place
is the inside of a throat
the walls are panting
like a lover once removed
and then some.
Tonight every wish is a piece of glass,
a weapon, an open wound
waiting to happen.
We've been awake long
enough to know better,
long enough to know hope stings
as it leaves the body like a last breath
returns as a broken bottle.

After so much history
it comes down
to a falling chandelier
glitter to shatter
a torn negligee
stained lace
a cheap thrill.

I think it's like driving
by an old apartment
knowing your key doesn't fit anymore.
It is that door,
the something hanging on the door
which we would never buy.
It is old cities
all their beauties
broken in battle.
It is a dying mare, rotting fruit,
it is *well enough alone*
and *not quite* all at once.
It is something
and something beyond that
more tender and terrible.
Don't you understand?
I couldn't have cared less.
I couldn't have cared less.

CARILLON

…not to disturb the slumbers of La Esmeralda;

the unfortunate creature would be awakened time enough to die.

—Victor Hugo

Bells ring of a dark-haired girl saying
her name sounds like metal breaking.
She dances like water moves, let me part
her (if only he'd said part with her).
What if the gypsy girl had kissed the priest?
If she spun slowly, faced him full-on.
What if she called his name just once and low?
Said something about pain and music,
a painted tambourine, the body's sway.
If he'd forgive her beauty, his desire?
Or if a priest could love a gypsy girl
the way one loves a firefly, a god,
a star, any sparkle in any sky.
Tenderly, and from a great distance.

RIVERSIDE DRIVING RAIN

after CD Wright, for Alabama: the girl with a ballroom heart

Wet-hot sidewalk. Dogmouth moist. Middle of the night walking to the gas station for ice cream, for peppermint patties and diet soda. Always hitting the wrong key typing the address and wrote instead rivers die. Rivers die. They do.

The geologist's garden. Flowerstone. Mosquitoville. Look away. *Look away.* A team with an abstract name. The balloon man on the corner. The crimson tide of tailights. Game days. Most days. *Coffee with you would be very heaven.* We hid inside. The habaneros. The multi-colored bells. The serranos.

Creatures of habit. Matchbox cockroaches. *Kittens, kittens everywhere, baby come look.* Ma'Cille's House of Miscelleny. A barbed-wire collection. A grove of bottle trees. *Too late and dark for you. Come over and we'll walk home together.*

Light brown overalls. Hand-delivered rainbows. On the fourth day he created the spider lily. Little Miss Firecracker with a heart the blue of hydrangeas lit up inside. A kickback of twilight. Why am I here? The Dibby. The Bear. The dead baby bunny called Luther: our sleepy warrior. Second-hand blankets. Thriftshop chairs. Babysteps. Babysteps. When we needed to march.

Four thousand packs of cigarettes later. A suede shirt the color of brownies. The sweetheartshaped torso inside. Kudzu and strawberries and fireants. Berries in the gully. Grown from a thorned memory plant. If I eat them will I die back into you?

The suicide laundromat. The medicinal smell of the belly. Where am I now? Watching so much blown straw and momentary confetti. Writing my umpteenth elegy for a downed-pilot, for that Riviera summer-once and us. Watching James and the Giant Peach. Watching out for the hyenas. Happy cologne. Heaven perfume.

The broken banjo the black cat played in the corner of the room. The outdoor pool where an Indian boy drowned himself two summers before. We tangled there. Chlorinated, inebriated from stale summer, our own ghostly hold. Cheap gin and sugarfree tonic. Scavenging. Dixiecup alcoholics. Rich days. Red velvet cakes. That loathesome watered-down cafe. *You're here because I love you.*

• • •

Where did I go? Moved to a town with a stutter in its name. The blue steel tree at the information kiosks. *The wayfinding tree never found me.* No matter, even the grackles look greasy and ungroomed. They know what I mean about morning and the minus signs of light that come through the blinds. Blades. Calling the landlord. This new life has already sprung a leak. Bringback is possible in myth. Who said that? *We'll walk home together.* Bringback is possible. That's it.

POEM FOR MY TAX-MAN

Mid-April Gripes:
Waist deep in it, what difference anyway?
We're up to our necks in expenses.

Many Happy Returns
Toast us then: a hundred hosannas
for our hello. A dust mote
for our farewell.

Next Earning Cycle:
Oh, L, we haven't lost a thing. Not
velocity. Not
volition. Not
time. We're a series
of gains and interest.
Everything savings. Everything
saved. The good investment.
Earnings and returnings.
No less than sign
a boomerang. No end
just dividends.

A decade from your last breath,

your recorded voice, a reading in Cincinnati,

where you open with a poem about Fresno

and living the kind of life that uses you up.

I can tell from your comments between poems

that these are your Salt Lake years, that maybe sometime

I passed you in the lower avenues. Walked through

a park where some lucky woman had loved

you just that afternoon.

I stammered when I spoke to you.

You're dead—ten years now—there's still

so much left of you and here, so much older

myself, two cities from the city

we both finally fled, your voice bounces

off the hardwood of my living room,

I'm surprised not to be sad: that you're dead

is not that astonishing anymore, that you lived

at all, another matter.

You said that Charles Wright wrote better of the spirit

than you ever could, "my poems are made of dirt

and grease" you explained. Larry, you're wrong,

your house is breath, your poems breathe

themselves into being: bright balloons,

using all their oxygen just to fill themselves up.

Let's wander through that pretty alley,
lollygaggers and derelicts
to the end. Faithful only
to this very last today
and the way you'll look
at the ground for the next
fallen hat and I'll jump
at the trees, one hand high-fiveing
the generous branches.
When we reach my street the one
with the name that sounds like
a German flower, a cab will round
the corner with the radio up, the windows
gushing: *When she speaks villages appear*
    and I will want to be that she
and you will think I am.

PHANTOM VENTRILOQUIST HAIKU

Each word alphabet soup
always someone else the chef
Just watch your mouth, Boy.

                    Do you think I feel
                    heard? I'm mute as you and then
                    some. After all I'm human.

Dumbest of all beasts.
Really. I'm your only voice.
I know how lacking.

                    Pursed lips, angry child,
                    my lap for a chair, my arm
                    for a spine. Listen:

Voicelessness suits you.
You're really no more dummy
Than every mortal.

                    Besides you're stuck here.
                    Slumped over and silent just
                    like me without you.

Read my lips, Lap Doll.
How your songs sound without me:

FURIOSO

I killed nothing on the day we met,
nothing on the day you called me off
like troops or the ledge, killed nothing but belief
the air that carried your scent across to me
didn't mean to give the molecules an extra shake.
Each time I disappeared into your arms
we protested war. What I had of sanctuary
cathedraled down your spine, the architecture:
Italianate, inviting, the narthex: cathartic, divine.
Even at the table where I could never
complete a meal, I could see the leftovers
in your eyes. You heard the pep rallies inside me,
arranged the silverware, the next banquet,
my skeleton inside your arms. I never slept
so soundly, so soon. Elsewhere, bombs fell,
ours was the friendliest fire. Somewhere
a radio plays over a spent battlefield
a woman's voice sultries into the burning wind
    If I touched myself the way you touched me
and I am thousands of miles from the scene
    If I held myself the way you hold me
but my shoulders shiver thinking she means you.
I meant to dress your wounds
then undress them.
No harm done in this late light
peignoir discarded and the green freedom
of fatigues. We soldiered on until dawn
and when we woke there was nothing
left of the nuclear family.

Here's my bumper sticker: Take me
to the movies, kiss me in the midst
of the apocalypse. What we haven't fought
hard enough for, we die against.

To hear her tell it took you there. She, risen from the grave,
and riding now, the green line, heading downtown for a date
she won't be keeping—years dead and still brimming
with her husband's words.
         the science of saying goodbye
         in bareheaded laments at night.

No-Zeus-he, but lashes the length of feathers
He blinked and flocks of birds burst from piñata trees.

She said the snow fell inside her. That passion asked her for a match,
then stood in the corner, smoking away her life.
         learn, from starlight,
         what its fire might suggest.

Like Leda, she had to take him in,
keep him lodged inside her for years.
For a long time she thought about the Osip
before the prison camp, and what it means to salvage,
and about salvation, since who was doing the saving
and who was getting saved changed every night.
That's kinky enough for a frozen Russian romance
about a woman whose name means hope and a man
who was his own nesting doll, his heavy winter coat,
next his shirt collar, then the beard, beyond that: the quiet
of his face, beneath that: brilliance, then so much
sadness—and she knows as a wife knows, that the last doll is rage.

There are final things she hasn't yet named:
the wooden concentric dolls of her husband's soul, the one

moment when everything yearned for is one
thing. Who could want so much and survive it?

Next stop Astor Place.

Nevermind the losing. The laying-him-down that last time,
how the soil seemed to her gleeful
to be holding him. How, holding herself steady,
she decided then to engrave him—syllable by syllable
into her bones. His otherwise-lost verses
and the nights she spent, memorizing
them all, so that they'd have to cut her to take
even one word away. The lightest of them
she floated into her bloodstream, like leaves,
liking the way they felt as they eddied
around her pulse. Her favorite poems she tattooed
onto her organs because the brambled
graffiti spelled him back to her.

He thinks in bone and feels with his brow

She wishes for him to have all that he desires: another winter, a wife to carry it in.

Say then, she did put his knowledge
with his power on. There are whole selves
she has left to her husband's charge, mothballed,
preserved. A naphthalene cologne streams from their clothes
and when he wanders in spirit-first, she can almost smell herself
a little wrapped around him, a little stopped in time.

She said she rides the train every day. Sit beside her if you can, listen and you'll hear the rustle
of them: Osip's poems sprawl like housecats on all the furniture inside her body.
Each breath makes a phrase swing in the branches of her lungs. Each step shuffles the order.

Once or twice in his life, a man is peeled away like an onion.
She only wanted to be the one to gather the spiraled remains,

to see to it, that nothing of him could ever be lost.

An empty boat drifts on the naked river.

Dawn for the last time, his voice curls out, turns into her like an icepick
formed of smoke, the tendrils of vowel sounds open
like little envelopes gentle in their tear, the consonants tune their instruments.
Her stomach tightens and her dead husband's name leaves her mouth in starling chaos.
Each time she spoke it, his name sent a secret to the roof of the mouth
Knowledge and power and the way to know him again by heart, by rhythm, by breath.

It's a dangerous thing to ignore

There's no packing for a journey with someone who contains all his destinations.
He is his luggage and all that it holds. Instead, she wishes for him one exquisite day, rain made
of diamonds, a paper cloud and a high wind to send it away.

To have such…regard for someone. You
can't know,
can't possibly imagine.

(You'd be surprised, Nadezdha.)

Next stop Canal Street.

Below ground she travels like a drug through the veins. She's remembering again:
she is shooting through him like lightning.

Maybe buy you a drink, help you move on?

Don't do it, Nadezdha, every man really is an un-Osip, their one dumb mouth moving toward
you like an injury, their lashlessness an affront and everyplace: *Mandelstam*
with his name like a hammered instrument. Hopeful man—fool,
if you could look into her, you'd understand.
Half-written litanies drape across her ribcage. A stray lament eyes you darkly from her liver.
Her insides are alace with his elegies. There's no room for anyone else inside her.

CHARM FOR INDUCING RAZBLIUTO*

for there should be one swarm of swallows add songbirds
                    as needed

at least one able to swallow the bitterness an untuned
piano

crumbs strewn on concrete the sidewalk's slap
            against soles

even lakes feel like cement when we fall

so far rocks in our hands a glass house
    each panel every pane blown from our own

breath

*Russian term for the feeling one has for someone s/he once loved but now does not

I am out drinking up shadows, of people in hats,
of trees, leafless are best, I like the stark cursive in my gut.
Bird shadows fly through me and right then, I'm back there
Salt Lake City, riding my bike through a flock
of blackbirds, so many, that for a second,
we're kind of flying together.

But not today. Today the birds are all shaky
and they fly through the shape of me
like I'm a cloud-shaped person.
I am walking to the petstore to see not birds
but the new fluorescent fish everyone's so worried about: Glofish.
Genetically engineered. Glofish.
Their bodies a living Vegas, shine
and turn, neon spelling themselves glofish
to the water red flash, red flash and zip by
a crazy barber pole, striped dark and lit
up transgenic message
that scares the bejesus
out of every God-fearing riverfish.

I am walking to the sandwich shop
and wishing for some fluorescence of my own.
A little blacklight and my blood
could be a visible circus.

I walk by four houses
with their televisions on.
The tv is the kind of glass box

aquarium for president fish
and war fish and terror warnings
that come in colors like crayons.
I keep them there like pets.

They are far away and today is close at hand.
Not every day is. Some days are birds bending
around your ribcage and taking off.
They light on a signpost and stare back.
I just read a poem about a plymouth
I wanted to drive away in.

you won't wander into the room where I keep you
and your sundry relics: the silkworms, cobwebs,
sawdust and the soda bottle—*beautiful*
because your mouth was once on it.

Marisol, I am waiting for you
to destroy me, one line
from the right book would do it
or ransacking the room where I keep you

filed pristine between your own perfect ribs.
You're just like that streetcorner guy
that whacks me with an umbrella
and then apologizes to the umbrella.

Marisol I'm sorry about that slanted rain
and I'm sorry about the whole sky rolled
over us steamroller-like, Marisol,
now reading the Russians makes me wistful

on the train from Brooklyn where GG falls in love
every five minutes   so GG he was happy
because at his gig the other night
someone gave him a slice of Grand Marnier cake

with little moon-grins of mandarin oranges.
Marisol you have been so pretty at the same time
as that fruitstand where they sell peacock blue
flowers you have been pretty

mean over macaroni but never wings,
wings make you happy like
I am made happy to drink too much
coffee and so much gets lost

on the trains between stations.
Marisol   you happened   then you stopped.
You have to believe in a world like that
even when it sweeps you away

ACKNOWLEDGMENTS

These poems have appeared, sometimes in slightly altered form, in the following journals:

The Allegheny Review, Alimentum, Amaranth, Anti, Bellevue Literary Review, Born Magazine, Café Review, Cantilever, Crab Orchard Review, Faultline, Florida Review, Hotel Amerika, Indiana Review, International Quarterly, Jabberwock Review, Madison Review, Margie, Melic Review, Mississippi Review, Mot Juste, Other Voices, Passages North, Pebble Lake Review, Poem, Memoir, Story, Poetlore, Saint Katherine Review, Slope, Southern Review, String Poet and *Quarterly West.*

The author wishes to thank the editors of: *A Face to Meet the Faces: An Anthology of Contemporary Persona Poetry* for reprinting "Pinocchio's Elegy for the Unreal."

With gratitude to Dana Curtis, and the whole fine crew at Elixir for selecting this book, taking such care with it and for their infinite patience.

My family, again, always, especially Evan George and Miranda Karina for all the wit and wonder. Steve Fellner for being Steve Fellner. Lesley Jenike and Cynthia Arrieu-King for collaborations in language and life. (Plus, sugar and tears.) Simone Muench: thank you for your poems. My colleagues and fine students (often, also friends) at Columbus College of Art and Design: I am honored to be in your midst. Jacqueline Osherow, Eleanor Wilner and Cindi Clum-Oppenheimer: with awe and affection. Special thanks to Kathrine Wright, and Stephanie Rogers for their great words and careful polishing of mine. Eliot Khalil Wilson, the ever-Bear of good spice and raisin tart, thanks for the life-long write-along and cheering-on.

The line *I'm satisfied and tickled too, just to be with you* in the dedication to this book is quoted from Mississippi John Hurt.

ARIANA-SOPHIA KARTSONIS teaches at Columbus College of Art and Design and serves as faculty advisor to Botticelli Literary/Art Magazine. Her collaborative chapbook: *By Some Miracle, a Year Lousy with Meteors*, written with Cynthia Arrieu-King, won the Dreamhorse Press Prize and was published in 2013, and another, *Aloha, Vaudeville Doll* was published in 2014 by Dancing Girl Press. Her previous collection *Intaglio*, winner of the Wick Poetry Prize, was published in 2006 by Kent State University Press.

POETRY

Circassian Girl by Michelle Mitchell-Foust

Imago Mundi by Michelle Mitchell-Foust

Distance From Birth by Tracy Philpot

Original White Animals by Tracy Philpot

Flow Blue by Sarah Kennedy

A Witch's Dictionary by Sarah Kennedy

The Gold Thread by Sarah Kennedy

Monster Zero by Jay Snodgrass

Drag by Duriel E. Harris

Running the Voodoo Down by Jim McGarrah

Assignation at Vanishing Point by Jane Satterfield

Her Familiars by Jane Satterfield

The Jewish Fake Book by Sima Rabinowitz

Recital by Samn Stockwell

Murder Ballads by Jake Adam York

Floating Girl (Angel of War) by Robert Randolph

Puritan Spectacle by Robert Strong

Keeping the Tigers Behind Us by Glenn J. Freeman

Bonneville by Jenny Mueller

Cities of Flesh and the Dead by Diann Blakely

The Halo Rule by Teresa Leo

Perpetual Care by Katie Cappello

The Raindrop's Gospel: The Trials of St. Jerome and St. Paula by Maurya Simon

Prelude to Air from Water by Sandy Florian

Let Me Open You A Swan by Deborah Bogen

Cargo by Kristin Kelly

Spit by Esther Lee

Rag & Bone by Kathryn Nuernberger

Kingdom of Throat-stuck Luck by George Kalamaras

Mormon Boy by Seth Brady Tucker
Nostalgia for the Criminal Past by Kathleen Winter
Little Oblivion by Susan Allspaw
Quelled Communiqués by Chloë Joan López
Stupor by David Ray Vance
Curio by John Nieves
The Rub by Ariana-Sophia Kartsonis
Visiting Indira Gandhi's Palmist by Kirun Kapur

FICTION

How Things Break by Kerala Goodkin
Nine Ten Again by Phil Condon
Memory Sickness by Phong Nguyen
Troglodyte by Tracy DeBrincat

LIMITED EDITION CHAPBOOKS

Juju by Judy Moffat
Grass by Sean Aden Lovelace
X-testaments by Karen Zealand
Rapture by Sarah Kennedy
Green Ink Wings by Sherre Myers
Orange Reminds You Of Listening by Kristin Abraham
In What I Have Done & What I Have Failed To Do by Joseph P. Wood
Hymn of Ash by George Looney
Bray by Paul Gibbons